Catechist's Guide

Praying with Young People

TIPS FOR CATECHISTS

Maureen Gallagher

PAULIST PRESS
New York / Mahwah, NJ

Cover & book design by Lynn Else

Library of Congress Cataloging-in-Publication Data

Gallagher, Maureen, 1938–
    Praying with young people : tips for catechists / Maureen Gallagher.
      p. cm.
    ISBN 978–0–8091–4401–3 (alk. paper)
    1. Prayer—Catholic Church. 2. Church work with young adults. 3. Catechists. I. Title.
    BV215.G35 2007
    248.3'2071—dc22

2007003050

Published by Paulist Press
997 Macarthur Boulevard
Mahwah, New Jersey 07430

www.paulistpress.com

Printed and bound in the
United States of America

Contents

Introduction: Praying

v

1. Creating

1

2. Relating

10

3. Dying and Rising

19

4. Welcoming

30

5. Affirming

40

6. Praying to and with Mary

48

7. Being a Disciple

61

iii

Introduction

PRAYING

Jesus was the effective catechist par excellence. He is our model today. We reflect upon how Jesus went about forming his disciples. We know that he was an inspiring teacher and that he taught his followers to pray. This book is primarily about helping young people to pray, but prayer is never seen as an isolated event. Prayer flows from life, nurtures life, and sustains us through life.

The *General Directory for Catechesis* (GDC) states that the definitive aim of catechesis is communion and intimacy with Jesus Christ (GDC 80). It names six tasks in the catechetical ministry: promoting knowledge of the faith, liturgical education, moral formation, teaching to pray, education for community life and missionary formation (GDC 85, 86). As the Directory notes, all these are interconnected.

"Communion with Jesus Christ leads the disciples to assume the attitude of prayer and contemplation....To learn to pray with Jesus is to pray with the same sentiments with which he turned to the Father: adoration, praise, thanksgiving, filial confidence, supplication and awe for his glory" (GDC 85). The Directory goes on to remind us that when catechesis is permeated with prayer, the entire Christian life reaches its summit (GDC 85).

What is prayer?

Prayer is the process of entering into conscious communication with God. Prayer recognizes that we have an ongoing relationship with a God who cares for us and wants us to be happy. Prayer is about presence, being present to a loving God. Saints have described their own experience of prayer as dialogue, as attentiveness, as intimate sharing.

God invites prayer. God desires to have an intimate and loving relationship with us. God welcomes us when we share our petitions, when we offer praise and thanksgiving, and when we seek reconciliation and mercy. The Directory reminds us, quoting from the Second Vatican Council on revelation, that "Revelation is that act by which God manifests himself personally to man (and woman). God truly reveals himself as one who desires to communicate himself making the human person a participant in his divine nature. In this way God accomplishes his plan of love" (GDC 36). The only way this divine relationship with God is realized is through prayer.

Prayer leads to conversion, to having a change of heart. Prayer opens the doors of mystery and beckons one into new levels of awareness. Prayer is communion with God.

People of prayer grow in charity and understanding of others. They let go of selfish ways and embrace others who may need them. Prayer keeps people on track as they travel the mazes of their faith journeys.

Prayer is often classified under three headings: vocal prayer, contemplative prayer, and passive prayer. Vocal prayer includes liturgical prayer, devotional prayer, prayers developed over the centuries, spontaneous prayer, and sung prayer. Vocal prayer is sometimes accompanied by gestures. In a liturgical setting vocal prayer often uses the Scriptures and formal prayers of the church. This book includes many examples of vocal prayer including suggestions for music and gestures.

Contemplative prayer is a process of reflection. It often uses imagination and is frequently referred to as meditation. Journaling is a way of recording reflective thoughts. In this book it is suggested that adolescents begin a prayer journal in which to record their prayers and their faith musings. The middle-grade children could begin using a journal also, but they will need more direction and time to do it.

In contemplative prayer, people use Scripture, spiritual reading, poetry, literature, and the beauties of nature to help them pray. Contemplative prayer leads to stillness and stillness leads to communion with God. People often use mantras in contemplative prayer to quiet themselves interiorly. Mantras are introduced in chapter 4 for the middle-grade children. However, they can be used at all levels, if they are explained in a simple way.

Throughout this book people are invited to reflect silently on the Scripture readings or the catechetical themes. The prayer suggested for the catechist is always one calling for quiet reflection. Catechists, too, would benefit from beginning or continuing to use a prayer journal.

Passive prayer is like the height of contemplative prayer, where the one praying is so receptive to the Lord's presence that he or she is deep with God. It is truly a mystical experience. Using vocal and contemplative prayer can prepare us for mystical prayer.

The Directory calls all Christians to look at the world from the perspective of faith. Prayer aids in this regard, for it helps Christians realize that: (1) all reality is marked by the creative activity of God, which communicates goodness to all; (2) the power of sin limits and numbs people; (3) the dynamism which bursts forth from the resurrection of Christ, the seed renewing believers, is the hope of a definite "fulfillment" (GDC 16). Prayer is the link between what is God's reality, the reality of all existence, and our awareness of it. Without that connection human beings are deprived of the consciousness of divine existence. Catechesis and prayer embody this world view.

Besides everyday prayer "catechesis is intrinsically bound to every liturgical and sacramental action. Frequently, however, the practice of catechetics testifies to a weak and fragmentary link with the liturgy and limited attention to liturgical symbols and rites" (GDC 30). *Praying with Young People* incorporates rituals and symbols used in liturgy in every chapter. It attempts to help children become familiar with them in a less formal prayer setting so that the symbolic actions will be more meaningful to them when they are celebrated in public liturgy. *Praying with Young People* uses elements of liturgical catechesis as it helps children to pray. It attempts to enable young people to understand the meaning of signs and gestures and educates to active participation, contemplation, and silence (GDC 71).

Every prayer exercise in *Praying with Young People* incorporates Scripture. The Directory calls studying and praying with Scripture the "eminent form" of prayer (GDC 63). The "Church desires that in the ministry of the word, Sacred Scripture should have a pre-eminent position" (GDC 127). The questions either presented in preparation for the proclamation of the word or following it, often call for us to use our religious imagination. This promotes greater integration of the Word of God into our life, into the fiber of our being. Prayer is not primarily an intellectual exercise. Certainly it involves thought processes, but it also involves emotional responses. Faith is discovered and nurtured in the imagination. *Praying with Young People* incorporates a traditional and healthy use of religious imagination.

Prayer is also related to justice. Justice is a constitutive element in the gospels. By praying with Scripture, justice and the actions of justice are integrated into prayer. "The Church desires to stir Christian hearts 'to the cause of justice' and to a 'preferential option for love of the poor,' so that her presence may really be light that shines and salt that cures" (GDC 17).

Researchers in education have discovered that different people learn in different ways. Scholars like Howard Gardner and David Lazear have identified seven or eight modes of human intelligence. They include "verbal/linguistic intelligence, which is related to the use of words, spoken and written; logical/mathematical intelligence, which encompasses scientific thinking, numbers, logic, and abstract recognition; visual/spatial intelligence, which includes visualizing objects, colors, pictures, images, etc; body/kinesthetic intelligence, which includes bodily movement; musical/rhythmic intelligence, which includes all aspects of music; interpersonal intelligence, which functions through person-to-person relationships; *intra*personal intelligence, which focuses on self-reflection and awareness of spiritual realities; nature-based intelligence, which includes learning from all aspects of nature."

Praying with Young People has included all the modes of human intelligence into various aspects of prayer. The verbal/linguistic and the logical/mathematical are present throughout the book and are the most common ways in which educators in the Western culture transmit knowledge. However, to really grow in faith one needs to use all the "intelligences." Visual/spatial is used any time an art project or photography is suggested. Body/kinesthetic is used when processions or skits are recommended. Musical/rhythmic intelligence is included in every prayer. Music, both reflective music and song, is vital to communal prayer. Interpersonal intelligence is seen when small groups are called for and projects are assigned that ask for group interaction. Such exercises are found throughout *Praying with Young People*. Intrapersonal intelligence is prompted when participants are given time for quiet reflection, usually with some questions to stimulate thought and imagination. It is important to use a variety of ways to pray when working with children as they all have strengths and preferred ways to approach things. There is no one best way to learn. There is no one best way to pray. All people have unique gifts for learning and praying. Our job as effective catechists is to keep providing multiple methods and resources for people to grow in faith.

Praying with Young People has three goals:

1. to empower the catechist to effectively lead children in prayer using multiple activities;
2. to assist young people to experience prayer as communication and bonding with God and one another;
3. to help young people see the connection between learning about God, being in communion with God, and living as disciples of Jesus Christ.

There are seven chapters in this book, each devoted to a major catechetical theme. The chapters have four sections. The first section is devoted to a theological reflection on the theme and invites the catechist to pray. The second section describes a catechetical session for young children based on the theme and closes with a participative prayer service. The third part explores the same theme for middle-grade children and culminates with an active prayer service. The fourth focuses on the adolescent and has activities and prayer suggestions based on the chapter theme for that age group.

While the theme is the same for the entire chapter, each section draws upon different Scripture passages and different activities. The Scripture and the activities can easily be adapted and used interchangeably for different age groups. *Praying with Young People* is designed to be a resource, not a recipe book. It may be adapted to various cultural settings and geographic settings. It can be used in family programs, as part of liturgical catechesis, with traditional programs, for summer Bible schools, and in catechist training programs.

It is hoped that these resources will enrich the faith life of all who use or adapt them.

1
Creating

IMMERSED IN FAITH

We believe that God created all that is and that we are called to participate in God's creativity. We are called to embrace the world and its creative process and continue to build the reign of God. Creation-centered spirituality calls us to praise and thank God for all of creation. It nudges us to see the wholeness of life—not life in little compartments. It provides us with a framework that says nothing is profane for those who know how to see.

Spirituality based on God's creativity is incarnational. It sees redemption as an integral part of divine creation, and it proclaims that all creation is permeated with the grace of God. Holiness is seen in the "everyday," in the "ordinary." Creation-centered spirituality leads one to see the "more" in life. The "more" is like the glue that connects all of life, or the lens that helps us to see the interconnectedness of all life.

Prayer is a means to see life differently and to be in communion with the divine. The goal of catechesis is to enable people to be in communion with Jesus Christ, to

1

be one with him. Prayer helps us slow down our lives, to see the beauty that is in us and around us, and to become more aware of God's presence. Prayer nudges us to serve others, to continue creating a more just and merciful world. Prayer stimulates the imagination so that faith may grow.

PRAYING AS THE CATECHIST

Choose something, such as a flower, a rock, a small branch, or a picture of a sunset. Take your Bible, light a candle, then pray Psalm 65:9–13.

Pray in praise and gratitude for God's creation. Name the beauty you see in the element of creation you have chosen to focus on. How is that beauty reflected in your life? How does that beauty enrich your life? How can you share this beauty with others? How are justice and creation related? Finish your prayer with "All creation bless the Lord."

HELPING YOUNG CHILDREN TO PRAY

1. Call the attention of young children to whatever elements from nature are readily available, such as fall leaves, wild flowers, small branches, pictures of beautiful flowers or landscapes. If possible, take them on a nature walk and let them draw signs from nature that they love.

2. Have children share their artwork or what they have brought as a sign of beauty from nature. Ask them what they like most about what they have chosen. (It could be the color, the texture, etc.)

3. Remind them that God is the source of all creation. God made the world and all that is in it. Expand on this according to the interest and age of the children. If appropriate, explain that God made plants with seeds so that we would always have flowers and greenery. We do not want children to picture God "up in heaven," making every single flower in a workshop!

4. Discuss how we are to care for nature and respect it. Talk about times when people do not respect nature by polluting or destroying what God has given us. Ask each child to describe what he or she can do to protect all the natural gifts God has given.

5. Prepare for and implement the prayer service.
   - Begin with an opening refrain from a hymn the children know.
   - Have children stand in a circle and hold their drawings.
   - Ask them to close their eyes and remember that God made all of creation. Invite them to be quiet inside themselves so they can praise God for all the wonders of creation.
   - Opening Prayer: God, our creator, you have given us all the beauty of creation. Help us to care for it and to remember you when we see beautiful things.

We ask this in Jesus' name, through the power of the Holy Spirit.

All: Amen.

- Read from the book of Genesis, 1:10–11, 24–25. Invite the children to pretend they are God and have them decide what they think is God's favorite element from nature (excluding people), and then tell why they chose what they did. (There are no wrong answers.)

- Pray a litany of praise. Include each child's drawing in the litany. Have the children respond, "God is great" (Ps 70:4). Examples:

  Lord we praise you for Marie's flower.

  All: God is great.

  Lord we praise you for Peter's butterfly.

  All: God is great.

- Closing Prayer: God, we are your children. We care for all of your creation. Bless us and our families. We pray in the name of the Father and of the Son and of the Holy Spirit.

  All: Amen.

HELPING MIDDLE-GRADE CHILDREN TO PRAY

1. Decorate the classroom with various symbols of the seasons of the year. Use calendar pictures or nature scenes.

2. Optional: Show slides or videos that have various beautiful images from nature. Have appropriate art materials such as construction paper, foil, colored pipe cleaners, markers, glue, and magazines available for the children to make a symbol of their favorite season. Encourage their creativity.

3. Discuss with the children how the seasons change each year. Ask what the particular signs of each season are and which ones each of the young people likes best. Have them explain why. Point out the challenges of each season. Invite them to describe what they can do to care for creation during their favorite season. Focus on how caring for creation is part of being a good steward of all God has made.

4. Discuss what one can do in each season as well as what one is limited in doing. Point out that the Wisdom literature in the Bible points to the rhythms of life. Distribute copies of the reading or put it on the chalkboard or newsprint. Have the young people discuss the meaning of the various phrases.

5. Prepare for and implement the prayer service.
   • Have several young people choose a hymn to use, such as "All Creatures of Our God and King" or "All the Ends of the Earth." Select two young people to read Ecclesiastes 3:1–4, alternating verses. Invite four other participants to prepare general intercession prayers thanking God for the seasons of the year as well as the seasons of our lives.

- Invite the young people to sit in a circle with their eyes closed. Play some reflective music.
- Light a candle. Open the Bible to the reading from Ecclesiastes. Decorate the classroom with any art-work the children have done.
- Opening Prayer: God, our loving creator, you have given us the seasons in which to reflect on various aspects of your glory. We see plants bloom and die; we plant crops and harvest them; we try to get rid of evil and be healed from sin; we laugh and we cry and through all of this we know you are our God. We praise you for all creation and most especially we thank you for giving us your son, Jesus Christ. We ask you to be with us as we gather in the name of Jesus through the power of the Holy Spirit.
  All: Amen.
- Proclaim Ecclesiastes 3:1–4.
  Invite the young people to discuss what God's favorite "time" or "season" might be. Ask them to explain their choices. (There are no wrong answers.)
- General Intercessions: invite them to share their petitions.
  Response: Lord, hear our prayer.
- Pray the Lord's Prayer.
- Close with an appropriate hymn.

HELPING ADOLESCENTS TO PRAY

1. Invite the young people to begin a special journal for their thoughts and prayers. A prayer journal will give them an opportunity to record personal questions or queries, such as, "I was wondering about…," or "What would it be like if…," or "I wonder what was really going on in Jesus' mind when he said…"

2. Design the classroom so that it is rich with photos or natural elements. Optional: Use video or internet images to create a display with scenes of natural beauty.

3. Have colored index cards, markers, a Bible, reflective music, and several live plants with flowers to create a prayerful environment.

4. Invite the young people to name their three favorite aspects of nature (animals, plants, sunsets, etc.). Tell why these things mean something to them. Ask them to describe how God is present to them when they are in beautiful natural settings.

5. Invite the young people to name three things made by human hands that reflect creativity. Discuss why these items are creative.

6. Encourage each student to name something they have created. What made it creative? Did it serve a practical function or was it something of pure beauty? Point out that beauty and creativity are found not only in the visual arts, but also in music, poetry, dance, and so on.

7. Note that when we are creative we are participating in a very special way in God's creative energy. God's

grace is nudging us, supporting us, and motivating us to be creative and to share in his divine life.

8. Ask each person to design a logo representing what creativity means to them. Draw the logo on a colored index card. On the other side of the index card have each student write a prayer that expresses gratitude to God for the gift of creativity in the world and in individuals. Encourage the participants to take their cards home and put them someplace where they can see them regularly, appreciate their creativity, and say the prayer. The logo and prayer can also be put in their prayer journal.

9. Prepare for and implement the prayer service.
   - Invite individuals to prepare the reading from Isaiah 40:28–31 and to choose appropriate hymns for the service, such as: "Glory and Praise to Our God" or "Praise to the Lord, the Almighty."
   - Opening Prayer: God, our creator, you have made us to share in your creative life here on earth. Empower us to use our gifts and talents to bring about your reign on earth. When we are tired and weary empower us with your creativity to continue on the journey. We ask this in the name of Jesus Christ and through the power of the Holy Spirit. All: Amen.
   - Proclaim the reading.
   - For reflection:
     God has called us to share in the divine creativity, for God is creator of the ends of the earth. But we

do grow weary. We wonder about our creativity. We tend to hide it under a bushel. Sometimes it is because we are too tired. Sometimes it is because we are too timid and don't have enough confidence in ourselves. We feel insecure. We don't want to look foolish. But this reading tells us that the creator of the ends of the earth will renew us, will lift us up on the wings of eagles, will sustain us so that we will run and not grow weary, we will walk and not faint. Think about a time in your life when you lacked confidence to be creative or were too tired to keep on trying. What is this reading saying to you? When have you felt God's support? Who are the people in your life who have helped you to grow in confidence? Who has helped you to be creative?

- Invite small group faith sharing based on the reading and the logos created above. A person might share his or her logo and then share a reflection on how hard it is to be creative because of weariness and lack of confidence.
- General Intercessions. Afterwards, invite them to share the prayer they wrote on the back of their index card, and after each prayer, respond: Lord, hear our prayer.
- Pray the Lord's Prayer.
- Offer a sign of peace.
- Close with a song.

2
Relating

IMMERSED IN FAITH

Our God is a relational God: the Father, the Son, and the Holy Spirit. The energy or the grace of the Trinity explodes in the world and invites us all to be part of the graciousness of God. We are baptized into God's life and called to emanate God's presence in all of our relationships.

As we pray and help others to pray, it is the energy of the Trinity that we touch and by which we are influenced. This grace connects us to the divinity, to the "more" in our own lives. It motivates us to be good stewards of the earth. Prayer allows us to realize the presence of God in the very fiber of our beings. Prayer unites us to each other and the community of God's people around the world.

Trinity is at the heart of who we are as a people. Trinity puts us in a relationship not only with God but with the universe and with all people. The Trinity links us with the cosmos. It beckons us from isolation. It demands more from us than individual contributions. It calls us to see the bigger picture in relationship to who we are as a people. It places responsibility on us to care for all creation and to continue to build God's reign on earth and beyond the earth.

Prayer helps us tap into the trinitarian energy of God. It raises our consciousness of the almightiness of God, while at the same bringing us to an intimate relationship with God, especially through Jesus Christ.

PRAYING AS THE CATECHIST

Light a candle and slowly make the sign of the cross, recalling your relationship with the Trinity. Pray and reflect upon John 14:6,7,26.

We are connected to the energy produced by the three persons in the Trinity, who are constantly relating to each other. We participate in the trinitarian relationship through our baptism. Imagine being caught up in this divine energy. What is it like? What is comforting about it? What is scary? What can you become because of this divine energy? What are you called to do because of this energy?

HELPING YOUNG CHILDREN TO PRAY

1. For each child, fold a piece of 12" x 18" construction paper in three equal sections, with the long edge at the top. On the first section have the children draw something or someone that God has created. On the second section invite them to draw a picture of Jesus

and others doing good things for people. On the last section draw people doing kind acts because the Holy Spirit is with them.

2. Discuss the drawings. Point out that there is one God, but three persons: Father, Son, and Holy Spirit. And that when we speak of the three persons in God, we are speaking of the Trinity.

3. Note that God wants us to have a wonderful relationship with him. Through baptism we have become brothers and sisters of Christ, sons and daughters of God. God also wants us to have good relationships with other people. Ask the children to name relatives or friends whom they love. Have them describe wonderful things other people have done for them. Invite them to name one thing *they* do to help others.

4. In each of the three sections on the reverse side of the Trinity triptych, have the children draw themselves helping another person. Have them share one of the drawings with the entire group.

5. Talk about how we honor God by making the Sign of the Cross. Demonstrate this. Have the children practice making the Sign of the Cross.

6. Prepare for and implement the prayer service.
   - Begin by singing a refrain of a hymn with which the children are familiar.
   - Opening Prayer: God our creator, you gave us your son, Jesus Christ, to show us how much you love us and to show us how to be good disciples.

Jesus sent us the Holy Spirit to be with us forever and to help us to be good. We thank you for the great gift of the Trinity in the name of Jesus and the Holy Spirit.

All: Amen.

- Reading: Matthew 3:16–17.
- Note that when we were baptized, the priest baptized us in the name of the Father and of the Son and of the Holy Spirit. Today we remember our baptisms when we became sons and daughters of God in a special way. We dip our hands in the holy water and make the Sign of the Cross.
- Have the children repeat the following prayer after you:

  God our Father, we thank you for giving us life and a beautiful world.

  God the Son, our brother Jesus, we thank you for becoming one of us and showing us how to love God.

  God the Holy Spirit, we thank you for helping us to be good followers of Jesus.

  Amen.
- Have the children name one thing they will do for someone else because they share in the life of the Trinity.
- Close the prayer service by singing the refrain from the same hymn with which you began.

HELPING MIDDLE-GRADE CHILDREN TO PRAY

1. To help children to connect to God in prayer remind them that God is a relational God. God is like a close-knit family—one family, but three persons, Father, Son and Holy Spirit. Explain that through baptism we all became part of God's family. We are called to pray as a community of people who praise and thank God for all God has done for us. Because God is a relational being, God wants us to be in relationship to each other and to the divine person who is God.

2. Write the passage from Psalm 47:1–2, 6–7 on the chalkboard or on newsprint.

3. Discuss the psalm. Ask: what are your favorite verses in the psalm, and why? Which person of the Trinity is the psalm praising? Now offer your own reasons for praising God. Note that it is the Holy Spirit who helps us to pray.

4. Optional: divide the participants into four groups and assign a part of the psalm to each group. Provide them with old magazines, calendars, or pictures that they can use to make a collage. Have each group write their verses on or below the collage. After this is completed, invite each group to discuss their collage in relationship to the psalm.

5. Optional: divide the participants into two groups. Give the first part of the psalm to one group and the

second to the other. Ask each group to come up with appropriate gestures to use when praying the psalm. Practice the gestures.

6. Prepare for and implement the prayer service.
   - Ask several young people to select appropriate music, such as "Holy God We Praise Thy Name" or "Holy, Holy, Holy! Lord God Almighty."
   - Invite several people to write prayers acknowledging each person of the Trinity in different petitions of the general intercessions. Include some petitions for other people's needs.
   - Ask several people to choose a reading, such as Luke 3:21–22 or John 1:29–34.
   - If option 4 was chosen above, use the posters to decorate the prayer space.
   - Light a candle and open the Bible to the reading to be proclaimed.
   - Begin with an opening hymn (one or two verses).
   - Opening Prayer: God our Father and creator, you gave us your son, Jesus Christ, as our greatest gift on earth. Jesus did not want to leave us orphans so he gave us the Holy Spirit to be with us for all time. Help us always to be grateful to you for your gifts. We ask this in the name of Christ our Lord and of the Holy Spirit, our Advocate.
     All: Amen.
   - Proclaim the gospel chosen above.
   - Allow time for quiet reflection.

- Pray the general intercessions.
  Response: Lord, hear our prayer.
- Pray the Lord's Prayer.
- Exchange a sign of peace.
- Close with the third verse of the hymn that was sung at the beginning of the prayer service.

PRAYING WITH ADOLESCENTS

1. Distribute copies of the passage from John 14:16–17 to each individual, or write it on the chalkboard.
2. Point out to the participants that the mystery of the Trinity should remind us that God calls us to be in relationship with one another and to share in divine life.
3. Use the following questions to stimulate discussion of the Scripture passage.
   - Where is each person of the Trinity in the passage?
   - What do "advocates" do? What is another name for an advocate?
   - To whom do the words "another Advocate" refer?
   - How was Christ an "advocate" for us?
   - What is the "Spirit of truth?"
   - What role does truth play in our lives?
   - When are you aware that the Spirit is living in you?
   - What does the Spirit empower you to do? How is this empowerment related to justice, mercy, or charity?

4. Quietly reflect on the Scripture passage. Use your prayer journal to record your thoughts. Ask the Holy Spirit to help you in one area of your life. Use a phrase such as the following to share your prayer during the prayer service: Holy Spirit, empower me to be more _____ as I go about my daily life being a disciple of Jesus Christ.
5. Prepare for and implement the prayer service.
   * Ask an individual to prepare to proclaim the reading studied above.
   * Invite several participants to choose an appropriate hymn for prayer such as: "Now Thank We All Our God" or "This Day God Gives Me."
   * Light a small candle that can easily be passed from one participant to another. Have the Bible enthroned prominently.
   * Gather the participants in a circle. Begin with the selected hymn.
   * Invite all to pray the Sign of the Cross.
   * Opening Prayer: God our Father, you gave us your Son, Jesus Christ, to be our advocate, our brother, and our savior. Empower us with the presence of your Spirit to be true disciples of Christ. We ask this in the name of Jesus through the presence of the Holy Spirit.
     All: Amen.
   * Proclaim John 15:16,17.
   * Invite all to reflect quietly on the Scripture passage.

- Pass the candle to each participant. Invite each person to pray individually his or her "Holy Spirit empower me…" prayer. All respond: Lord, hear our prayer.
- Invite all to stand and pray the Lord's Prayer.
- Finish by singing an appropriate hymn.

3

Dying and Rising

IMMERSED IN FAITH

Jesus' cry on the cross—"My God, my God, why have you forsaken me?" (Mark 13:34)—reminds us of the times when we feel abandoned by our friends and even our God. The angel's message: "He has been raised; he is not here. Look, there is the place they laid him. But go tell his disciples and Peter that he is going ahead of you to Galilee; there you will see him, just as he told you" (Mark 16:6,7), points to the new life Jesus Christ brought to all of us by being raised by God from the dead.

Our faith sustains us as we go through many "death-resurrection" experiences in our lives. We lose loved ones. We lose jobs. Relationships are fractured. Dreams go unrealized. Life at times seems impossible. In other moments life is on the upswing and joy abounds. The birth of a new baby brings hope. The death of a spouse brings sorrow and a profound sense of loss. One of the graces of our Christian faith is our belief that God is with us through the dark days, through all the many kinds of death we

19

experience. The struggles associated with loss and pain are often the seeds of new life and hope.

Nowhere is this more apparent than in the story of Archbishop Oscar Romero. He was martyred on March 25, 1980 because he spoke out for the poor and against the injustice promulgated by the government of El Salvador. He was the "voice of the voiceless." He knew his life was in danger. But he also believed that if he were to die, he would not die in vain. He said, "If they kill me, I will rise again in the Salvadoran people." Today many people realize that he gave his life as a "seed of liberation." Young people who were not even born when Archbishop Romero was alive have embodied his spirit and continue his work to bring dignity to the lives of those who live in poverty.

Prayer sustains us in our darkest moments. It is through prayer that we are fortified with hope. It is through prayer that we can survive when only the bleakness of life surrounds us. Prayer diminishes the isolation associated with the many "deaths" we experience in life. Prayer also gives us a way to express the "Alleluia moments" in life when we are surrounded by joy, satisfaction, success, and exuberance.

PRAYING AS THE CATECHIST

Light a candle as a sign of Christ's resurrection. Reflect on Romans 6:4.

Reflect on times that you have suffered from depression, loss, sorrow, pain, or disillusionment. What were the tiny lights at the end of the tunnel? What elements of prayer were most important to you? How did your faith sustain you through those difficult times? Who were the people who walked with you? How can you help those you catechize deal with the "dying and rising" that is part of daily life?

PRAYING WITH YOUNG CHILDREN

1. Ask the children to name signs of life that bring them joy. These signs might be people, things, or events. Have them tell you why these things make them happy.
2. Optional: Have the children cut out magazine pictures that remind them of life and then paste their selections on poster board under this quote: "I came that they may have life and have it abundantly" (John 10: 10).
3. Discuss the positive signs of life that they have seen in nature or in pictures. Talk about how good God is and how God cares for us. Discuss happy moments and times of sadness (death of someone they loved, or a pet, a disappointment, sickness, etc.). Note that it is okay to be sad, and that all people have times when they are very sad.
4. Prepare for and implement the prayer service.
   - Place an open Bible near a lighted candle, and a picture of something beautiful in the prayer setting.
   - Begin with an opening song that the children know, such as "The Lord is Good to Me."
   - Make the Sign of the Cross with the children, inviting them to dip their fingers in a bowl of blessed water.

- Opening Prayer: God, you are always with us. You love us when we are happy and when we are sad. Help us to pray to you in thanksgiving when we are happy; help us to pray to you for strength when we are sad. We ask this in the name of Jesus our brother and friend and of the Holy Spirit. All: Amen.
- Proclaim the following passage:
  "I came that they may have life and have it abundantly" (John 10:10).
- Discuss the meaning of the passage by tying it to the previous discussion. Remind the children that God is with them whether they are happy or sad, and that God never leaves them.
- Ask them to name one thing they can do to make people happy.
- Ask them to respond to the following litany, or to one you have written, based on your discussion with them.
  Response: Lord, we thank you.
  God, we thank you for flowers.
  God, we thank you for the sun and rain.
  God, we thank you for giving us people who love us very much.
  God, we thank you for giving us people who help us when we are very sad.
  God, we thank you for our friends.
  God, we thank you for the wonderful food we eat every day.

God, we thank you for heaven and earth.

God, we ask you to always be with us, especially when we are sad.

For all the things in our hearts, God we thank you. Amen.

- Repeat the hymn used at the beginning of the prayer service.

PRAYING WITH MIDDLE-GRADE CHILDREN

1. Introduce the theme of the communal prayer by discussing the "death-and-resurrection" mystery of Christ. Note how Christ died so that we could share new life and not be slaves to sin. Point out that we experience many kinds of "deaths" in our lives: death to dreams, death of loved ones and pets, disappointments in ourselves and our performances, sickness that keeps us from being our best selves, and so on. Elicit from the participants as many examples of the "deaths" we experience in life as you can. List these on a chalkboard or newsprint.

2. Highlight that the "deaths" we experience often leave us sad or depressed and make us want to quit. Life can seem so hard. Focus on the fact that as Christians we have hope because Christ through his death and resurrection gave us a reason to believe that life will get better and that all is not lost.

3. Write the word HOPE vertically on the chalkboard or newsprint. Note that hope is the virtue that helps us to keep going when the going gets tough. Hope bridges the gap between death and resurrection. Hope pushes us from dying to living. Note that we are called to be a hopeful people and to live hope-filled lives.

4. Invite the young people to discover words associated with each letter of the word *hope* that points to the meaning of hope. Examples: **H:** happiness, holiness, helping hands; **O:** opportunity, openness, one, oneness; **P:** partner, pal, people; **E:** excited, energy, enlighten. Then ask them to work in groups of two or three to create sentences describing hope, using some of the words they generated. Example: Hope is looking for an opportunity to extend a helping hand to people in need.

5. Explain that the cycles of death and resurrection are celebrated by the church through the liturgical year. Each liturgical year begins with Advent in anticipation of the birth of Jesus Christ, with the hope of Christ coming anew into our hearts. Shortly after the Advent-Christmas cycle, Lent follows. Lent is the time when we focus on prayer, fasting, and almsgiving in order to prepare for Good Friday, when we commemorate Christ's death, and Easter Sunday, when we celebrate his resurrection. After the Easter-Pentecost cycle we are back to "ordinary time" when we return to hearing the stories of Jesus' public life

proclaimed. Discuss the importance of the liturgical year. Point to how it is a sign of hope and renewed expectation that each year we will grow to be more faith-filled disciples of Jesus Christ. Ask the children to imagine what it would be like not to celebrate Christmas and Easter every year.

6. Distribute copies of the following Scripture quotes or put them on the chalkboard or newsprint for all to sec: Acts 24:15–16; Romans 5:2; Romans 8:25; Romans 15:13.

- After a brief discussion of the meaning of each passage, invite the children to work in small groups. Each group will select its favorite passage and prepare to proclaim it in the prayer service. If several groups choose the same passage, suggest they proclaim it together as a group.

- Invite several participants to choose an appropriate hymn for the prayer service, such as "Alleluia! Alleluia! Let the Holy Anthem Rise" or "Blest Are They" or "Lord of the Dance."

7. Prepare for and implement the prayer service.

- Light a wax candle or an electric candle near the enthroned Bible.

- Make the Sign of the Cross.

- Opening Prayer: God the God of hope. Enable us to be hope-filled people. You gave us the gift of hope at baptism. Help us to realize that even when things are not going well, you are with us and your spirit is breathing hope into our lives. Empower us to offer each other hope as we face our struggles in life. We ask this through Jesus Christ our Lord and friend.

All: Amen.

- Liturgy of the Word: Each group proclaims the Scripture passage chosen from above. Allow time for reflection.

- General intercessions:

  Response: Lord, give us hope.

  For the times we feel hopeless…

  For the times we are discouraged…

  For the times we struggle to do good…

  For the times we neglect to be hope-filled for others…

  For the times we ignore the promptings of the Holy Spirit in our lives…

- Stand and pray the Our Father.
- Offer each other a sign of peace.
- Sing a final verse to the hymn sung above.

PRAYING WITH ADOLESCENTS

1. Adolescents have enough of their own history to begin to reflect on the death-and-resurrection mystery in their own lives. They experience emotional swings that can either leave them in the depths or cause them to be riding the clouds. However, their experiences are limited. They often have no sense of the finality of death. Suicide may be perceived as a

way to "get even" or "get attention." Many adolescents have experienced the death of a peer from an incurable disease or a tragic accident. Some have experienced the divorce of their parents or the death of a parent or grandparent. They all have experienced the disappointments that come from apparent failures in various kinds of performances. By using the "life-death" theme in prayer, adolescents get a chance to articulate their experiences and their fears.

2. To begin the discussion leading to prayer consider using some of following questions. Invite the young people to journal about them before sharing.
   - What is the worst thing that ever happened to you?
   - What is the best thing that ever happened?
   - Think of something good that eventually came out of something bad. What happened? What was good?
   - Invite the participants to do the following activity in small groups. Emphasize that they are to imagine they are Jesus in the exercise. Do a search of Luke's Gospel. Make a list of ten positive things that happened to you (Jesus) in your "public life." Save the resurrection for number 10. Make a list of all the disappointments or "little deaths" that happened to you (Jesus) in your public life. Save the crucifixion for number 10. Have each group find three positive and three negative things that happened to Jesus and that are similar to their own experiences.

3. Distribute copies of the quotation from Romans 5:1–5, or post it on chalkboard or newsprint for all to see.

   Name experiences where suffering produces endurance, and endurance character, and character hope. Who are some people you know who have suffered and become stronger as a result of their struggles? What can we do to help people who are enduring suffering?

   Have the young people work in groups of two or three to develop a slogan related to hope and dealing with disappointments, sickness, and even death.

   Optional: Make a poster with the slogan on it.

4. Prepare for and implement the prayer service.
   • Prepare a prayer environment where the Bible is enthroned and a candle is lit.
   • Invite several people to help choose the opening song reflecting hope or the death-and-resurrection theme, such as "Only in God," "Psalm of Hope," or "The Love of the Lord."
   • Choose one or two readings from the following (or choose another appropriate reading): Romans 6:3–4; Romans 6:6–10; 2 Thessalonians 1:3–4; John 20:19–23. Invite several to prepare to proclaim the Scriptures.
   • Invite participants into a circle and begin the selected hymn.
   • Opening Prayer: God, you are always with us through your Spirit. Enable us to accept the

crosses that come into our lives as Jesus accepted his disappointments and ultimate crucifixion. Be with us in our times of suffering. Make your presence known also in times of joyful celebration. Support us through the life, death, and resurrection of your son, Jesus Christ, our Lord, friend, and redeemer. We ask this in his name and through the power of the Holy Spirit.

All: Amen.

- Proclaim the reading(s) chosen above.
- Provide time for quiet reflection based on the following question: How can I "be a child of the resurrection" with my friends when they are down or discouraged?
- Invite each person to offer a prayer of petition such as in the following format:

  Lord, be with me when I am down and discouraged...Lord, hear our prayer.

  Lord, help me to reach out to others who are going through hard times...Lord hear our prayer.
- Have all stand and pray the Lord's Prayer.
- Invite all to share a sign of peace.
- Sing the final verse of the hymn chosen above.

4
Welcoming

IMMERSED IN FAITH

Part of our Judeo-Christian value system has always
included hospitality. When God appeared to Abraham in
the form of three strangers, Abraham hurried to provide
food and drink for them with the help of Sarah, his wife. It
was in this welcoming encounter with God that Sarah and
Abraham were promised a son (Gen 18:1–15). Later hospitality became encoded in the Jewish law (see Lev
19:33–34). In the Letter to the Hebrews (13:12) we are
also reminded to be hospitable. In the Letter to the Romans
Paul reminds the early Christians, "Contribute to the needs
of the saints; extend hospitality to strangers" (Rom 12:13).
In the First Letter to Timothy, Paul includes hospitality as
one of the characteristics needed by a bishop (1 Tim 3:2).
This is repeated in the Letter to Titus (Titus 1:8). Saint
Peter reiterates the need for hospitality, saying, "Be hospitable to one another without complaining" (1 Pet 4:9).

The sacrament of baptism is the sacrament of welcoming, of sharing new life. At baptism we are initiated into a
community that is on a pilgrimage to God and on the way

is building the reign of God. One of the first things the early Christian community did was to share food with those in need—an exercise in hospitality (Acts 2:43–47).

Hospitality remains very important today, since we live in a diverse culture. The ethnic, religious, and economic diversity of modern society compels us to embrace diversity and offer hospitality to others in ways that go beyond traditional understanding. Aiding the homeless, welcoming new immigrants, helping people find jobs, sharing life and faith—these are some of the ways in which a Christian demonstrates hospitality.

Prayer permits us to slow down our lives, so that we can become more aware of the great need for hospitality and welcoming. Providing refreshments for meetings is a small gesture of hospitality that sets a welcoming tone, creates a home-like atmosphere, and sends a message that people are important. Through prayer we are also made conscious of the larger need for hospitality, for providing food and shelter to the homeless, for welcoming new people into both the civic community and the church community, for making meals for the ill, and so forth. Hospitality in all its forms is the mark of a Christian. Prayer sustains us and helps us to become aware of the need to reach out to others.

PRAYING AS THE CATECHIST

Sit in a quiet place. Light a candle to recall the presence of the Spirit who helps us to pray. Using the Scripture cited above, reflect on the passages that mean the most to you.

Recall a time when someone offered you hospitality, went out of his or her way for you. What was it like? What did you learn about yourself? The other person? Remember when you had an opportunity to offer hospitality to another. What was that like? What were the risks involved? On what level is the catechetical ministry one of hospitality? How do you offer hospitality in your catechetical ministry?

HELPING YOUNG CHILDREN TO PRAY

1. Explain that sometimes children move into our neighborhoods and enter our schools and do not know anyone. What would it be like to go to school or to church and not know one person? What can we do to be welcoming? What is hard about doing this?
2. Focus on the fact that Jesus loves all children and wants them to be happy. Jesus wants us to do all that we can to welcome other children as our friends.
3. Optional: Have the children make up a skit in which, in the first act, a new child comes to school and is rejected. No one will eat with the new student at lunch or play with him or her at recess. Go on to the second act in which other children invite the child to sit at lunch with them and play with them at recess. Ask which act is the one that Jesus would like? Have them explain why.
4. Prepare for and implement the prayer service.
   - Begin by singing a hymn the children know.
   - All make the Sign of the Cross.

- Opening Prayer: God, our creator, you have given us our parents to take care of us. Help us to reach out to others and be kind to them. We ask this through our Lord, Jesus Christ, our brother and friend and through the Holy Spirit. Amen.
- After lighting a candle, read 1 John 3:18.
- If the children prepared a skit, invite them to do it as a response to the reading. Discuss the skit in connection with the reading. If you are not using the skit, ask the children to talk about how they show that they love other people. Optional: Have them close their eyes and imagine that they sat on Jesus' lap when he invited the children to come near him. What would they say to Jesus? What would Jesus say to them? Invite them to thank Jesus in their hearts for loving them.
- Have the children repeat the above reading after you.
- Pray the general intercessions.

  Response: Lord hear our prayer.

  Give me strength to help others in need…

  Help me reach out to new kids in my neighborhood and at school…

  Help me to share my toys with others who do not have them…

  Jesus, help me to be like you in all I do.
- Stand and offer each other a sign of peace.
- Sing a closing hymn.

HELPING MIDDLE-GRADE CHILDREN TO PRAY

1. Discuss with the group the value of welcoming others or offering hospitality to them. Ask if any of them have moved from one place to another. Have them describe how it felt not to know anyone. Ask them to discuss how they initially got adjusted to a new neighborhood and school.

2. Continue the discussion by pointing out how some people, despite having been in the same school or neighborhood for many years, still feel isolated from the rest of the community. Discuss the reasons for this and invite the students to suggest ways to make such people feel more welcome. Note how Jesus would treat such people. Give the example of Zaccheus, who was friendless and disliked because of his job. Jesus wanted to know Zaccheus better and so invited himself to Zaccheus' home. He welcomed Zaccheus because he saw a lot of good in him that others did not see.

3. Optional: Invite the students to work in small groups and make a poster listing ten ways for middle-grade children to offer hospitality to other classmates or other children in school. Have them compare their posters and discuss the implications of being hospitable.

4. Prepare for and implement the prayer service.

- Write on the board: "God Has Welcomed Us into God's Family. We are Called to Welcome Others into Our Friendship Groups and into Our Families."
- Invite the young people to select a hymn or use the hymn they wrote above. Possible selections include: "Gathered as One" or "We Are Many Parts."
- Assign someone to proclaim the reading (Luke 19:1–10).
- Invite participants to stand in a circle. Note that a circle is a symbol of unity and protection. When the early settlers were traveling in covered wagons, they would arrange the wagons in a circle for protection. Point out to the group that circles symbolize inclusiveness. Everyone is part of the circle.
- Begin with the opening hymn.
- Opening Prayer: God our loving Father, you love all of us. You wish each of us to love others and not exclude anyone from our circle of friendship and concern. Give us strength to reach out to others and extend the hand of friendship and hospitality. We ask this through Christ our Lord.
  All: Amen.
- Proclamation of the Gospel reading.
- Invite the participants to do some faith sharing. Use the following questions or other appropriate ones to stimulate their discussion.
  How do you imagine Zaccheus felt when Jesus said he was coming to dinner? Have you ever felt like that? When?

Explain the risk Jesus took by telling Zaccheus he was coming to dinner at his house. Have you ever taken a similar risk?

Why is it hard at times to be inclusive in relationships with classmates?

What does being inclusive or hospitable to all have to do with my faith?

What is one thing I will do to be welcoming or hospitable to others?

Incorporate your ideas into the general intercessions using the following format:

God help me to _____, for this I pray to the Lord...

All: Lord hear our prayer.

- Pray the Our Father together.
- Offer a sign of peace to everyone in the circle.
- Sing the final verse of the opening song.

HELPING ADOLESCENTS TO PRAY

1. Introduce the theme of welcoming, hospitality, and inclusivity by having the young people reflect on their own experience of being included and welcomed as part of a group. Encourage them to share both positive and negative experiences they have had. Note that being hospitable is one aspect of including people. Relate this to the Scripture passages cited at the beginning of this chapter.

2. Point out that being welcoming, inclusive, and hospitable does not mean that all will want to become one of your best friends. There will always be people with whom you will be close, and others who will be just friendly acquaintances. Although not all will be your best friends, you should not exclude people from having a positive relationship with you, not isolate people, or form cliques where only the "in" group can relate to you. To be exclusive is to be unjust.

3. A wreath is a good symbol for wholeness, unity, and inclusivity. Use a green wreath to demonstrate the unity of the parts as well as the diversity that gives the wreath its richness and beauty. Note how symbolically a wreath, an endless circle, can remind us of infinity and the eternal. A wreath can be a sacred symbol that connects us to one another and to the grace of God, which binds the wreath together.

4. Distribute little strips of white paper to each person. Ask everyone to write the names of each of their friends on these strips of paper, fold the slips of paper in half so that the names are not showing, and place them on the wreath. When this part of the activity is finished, give each one small strips of colored paper. Ask everyone to take two pieces of the paper and write the names of two people to whom they will reach out and be hospitable to in the next week. Have the students fold the slips in half so the names are not showing and include these on the wreath.

5. Comment appropriately on the wreath that now has the names of "best friends" as well as people who will be included in some way in the lives of the people gathered.

6. Prepare for and implement the prayer service.
   - Have several participants choose an appropriate hymn such as "All Are Welcome" or "Gathered as One."
   - Invite someone to prepare to proclaim the reading from Ephesians 4:1–6.
   - Place a bowl of water in the center of the wreath. Gather the participants in a circle around the wreath they have just decorated.
   - Sing the opening hymn.
   - As we begin our prayer, let us sign ourselves with the waters of baptism as we recall first being initiated into the Christian community. (Invite all to come forward and make the Sign of the Cross using the water in the center of the wreath.)
   - Opening Prayer: God of unity, God of understanding, empower us to be people who include others and work with others to continue to create your reign on earth. Be with us when we lack the courage to break out of our comfort zone and reach out to others. Strengthen us to follow the example of your Son, Jesus, who reached out to all kinds of people and befriended many who were ignored by others. Bless our lives and our struggles. We ask this in the name of Christ our Lord and brother.
     All: Amen.

- Proclaim the reading.
- Silent reflection based on the question: What can I do to foster unity, inclusivity, and hospitality among my friends?
- Invite each person to contribute a prayer of petition based on his or her reflection. Use the following or a similar formula: God of unity, strengthen me to _____ so I can be a sign of your presence and concern for others. Let us pray to the Lord. All: Lord, hear our prayer.
- Close with the Lord's Prayer.
- Exchange a sign of peace.
- Sing a stanza from the opening hymn.

5
Affirming

IMMERSED IN FAITH

Jesus affirmed people. He was always telling them, "I see more in you than you see in yourself." He saw the "more" in Peter, especially his leadership qualities, despite his impulsiveness. He gave Peter time and space to "grow" because of all the good he saw in him. He recognized the compassion in Mary Magdalene and affirmed her generosity. He knew that women were just as capable of hearing the Word of God and responding to it. He believed the Samaritan woman was capable of both understanding and spreading the Good News.

While Jesus saw and affirmed the goodness in people, he also challenged duplicity. He had little time for superficial people. He preferred to work with people who were open to new ways of thinking, people who could make the connection between the God of their ancestors and himself. He counted on people to be honest, to be generous, to make a difference. He saw himself on a journey and affirmed others who were willing to journey with him. These were the people who witnessed his death, his resurrection, and the sending of the Spirit, who is still with us today. Because the Spirit has united us to Christ, we are the people he is affirming and counting on today. We are the ones who are on a journey, the journey of discipleship.

Prayer prompts us to reflect on how much God loves us, affirms us, supports us, forgives us, and shows us mercy. God's care and concern for us is dramatically witnessed in Scripture. Using our religious imaginations, we can unleash God's affirmative power and hear God speaking in the Scriptures as if they were written for us today, both to us as individuals and to our communities. What is God affirming in you? What do you think God is challenging you to do?

PRAYING AS THE CATECHIST

Jesus affirms people who reflect his values. He tells stories about people who are on the right track to further the reign of God. For instance, in the story of the prodigal son (Luke 15:11–32), Jesus affirms both the son who comes home begging for forgiveness and the father who embraces him. Jesus supports the actions of the good Samaritan (Luke 10:25–37) who goes out of his way to help someone in trouble. In the Martha and Mary story (Luke 10:38–42), Jesus affirms Mary, who believes she can be a true disciple by listening and absorbing all Jesus has to teach. Jesus acknowledges people who "hear the word of God and obey it" (Luke 11:28), for they are truly blessed.

Use one of the Scripture passages above to reflect upon the value of affirming others. Think of the power you have experienced by being affirmed. Take some time to become more aware of how you can better affirm others in your life and in your ministry. Helping others to have healthy self-esteem is like giving them a priceless gift. One way to do this is by genuinely affirming what you see in others. Make a list of ways you can affirm others, describing exactly what you are affirming in them. Affirm good deeds, good questions, good ideas, rather than clothes or material things. Close your prayer by thanking God for the wonderful affirmations you have had in your own life. Ask for a new awareness of how affirming you can be of others.

HELPING YOUNG CHILDREN TO PRAY

1. Discuss with the children how nice it is to hear a good word, a compliment, an affirmation. Give examples: "Thank you for helping me." "I love it when you do things without being asked." "I like the way you draw." "You are such a good reader." Note how each of us wants to hear nice things about what we are doing and what other people are doing.

2. Make a list on the chalkboard of good things to do and good things to say to others. Ask which of them might be difficult to do or say. Why are they difficult?

3. Talk about saying "thank you," and why it is important to say it. How do you feel when someone thanks you for something? What is your impression of the

person who lets you know that he or she appreciates you?

4. Talk about how Jesus liked it when people were grateful. Tell the story of the ten lepers in your own words, based on the gospel to be used in the prayer service below. Explain that leprosy was a very serious illness at the time Jesus lived on earth and that there were no medicines then to control it. Lepers had to live away from their families because they could give the dreaded disease to those with whom they came in contact. Discuss how the person in the story said "thank you" to Jesus. What did that show about the person? Have each child name one person to whom they are grateful and describe why.

5. Optional: On poster paper write the words "Thank you" with big open letters so the children can fill them in with colored crayons or markers. Use the poster to decorate the prayer space.

6. Prepare for and implement the prayer service.
   • Choose an appropriate song for the children to sing as they begin the prayer service.
   • Opening Prayer: God our creator, you have given us Jesus, your Son, to tell us about you and to help us act as you would like us to act. Be with us as we learn more about you. We ask this in the name of Jesus Christ, our Lord and brother.
     All: Amen.
   • Explain that the children are going to hear a story from the Bible about the ten lepers. Note that this

is not just a story about the past, but that Jesus is speaking to them today. Tell them that at the end of the story you are going to ask them what message Jesus is giving them today.

- Proclaim Luke 17:11–19.
- Ask them their opinions on the message of the story of the lepers. Reinforce the need to say "thank you" to others. Ask them to recall whom they are going to thank, and for what they want to thank them.
- Close by praying: Glory be to the Father, and to the Son and to the Holy Spirit. Amen.

HELPING MIDDLE-GRADE CHILDREN TO PRAY

1. Have the children think of positive words that make people happy and negative words that make people sad. Write these on the board.
2. Discuss the impact words have on people. Note how nice it is to be told "thank you," to be complimented, to be held in high esteem. Demonstrate how words do that. Also talk about the negative effect of words. Give examples of "put-down" humor. Talk about words that hurt, words that do not respect human dignity.
3. Point to these words of Jesus: "If you continue in my word, you are truly my disciples; and you will know the truth, and the truth will make you free" (John 8:31–32).

Write the following sentences on the board:

"I am the bread of life" (John 6:35).

"I am the light of the world" (John 8:12).

"I am the gate for the sheep" (John 10:7).

"I am the way, the truth, and the life" (John 14:6).

Ask them to spend quiet time choosing the "I am" sentence that appeals to them the most.

4. Prepare for and implement the prayer service.

- Have them choose an opening hymn such as "Now Thank We All Our God" or "Christ Be Our Light."

- Opening Prayer: God our creator, you gave us your Son Jesus and his words to bring us new life. Help us to live by his words. We ask this in his name, Jesus, Christ, our Lord and redeemer. All: Amen.

- Liturgy of the Word.
  Have each person stand and proclaim the "I am" sentence he or she has chosen, along with its meaning or personal significance.

- Response: Jesus, our friend and brother, help us to remember that you are the bread of life, the light of the world, the gate for the sheep, and the way, the truth, and the life. Be each one of these things for us.

- Pray the Lord's Prayer.

- With a branch and holy water, bless the young people, saying: "May you go forth and remember your baptism in the name of the Father and of the Son and of the Holy Spirit."

HELPING ADOLESCENTS TO PRAY

1. Discuss the effect of words in our lives. Invite the young people to gather in small groups. Ask each group to come up with three positive phrases they love to hear, as well as three negative phrases they dread hearing.

2. After about fifteen minutes invite the small groups to share their discussions. Write their words on the board in two columns: one for positive words and one for negative words.

3. Invite the participants to recall some of their favorite music. What are some of the words in the music? List them on the board. Discuss whether they have a positive or negative effect on the listeners. Ask about why these songs are so popular, especially if they have a negative effect.

4. Divide the participants into four small groups. Provide each with a copy of the New Testament or a copy of Romans 1:8–15. What are the positive phrases in the passage? Describe the tone of the passage. Have each group rewrite the passage, preserving the basic meaning but using contemporary images and language. The students should copy the rewritten passages into their prayer journals.

   Invite each group to share its "rewrite" with the other groups. Ask each student to think about how he or she does some things in daily life that Paul did, then share their responses.

5. Prepare for and implement the prayer service.

- Have the young people choose an opening song such as "Come Let Us Sing with Joy to the Lord" or "Resuscito" or "Whatsoever You Do." Write the passages from Romans 8:28 and Romans 8:31 on the board.
- Open with the selected song.
- Opening Prayer: God our creator, you gave us your Son, Jesus Christ, who helps us to understand your word and whom we follow in happiness. Empower us to study and reflect on the word of the Lord in order to be more faith-filled disciples. We ask this in the name of Jesus, the Lord. All: Amen.
- Proclaim the passage from Romans.
- Invite quiet reflection on these passages. Pray in your heart to God, thanking him for being "for us." Ask that God will continue to strengthen your faith so that you can truly believe that all things work together for good.
- Stand and pray the Lord's Prayer.
- Invite all to extend a sign of peace to each other.
- Close with the final verse of the opening hymn.

6

Praying to and with Mary

IMMERSED IN FAITH

From the earliest times, the church has been devoted to Mary, the mother of Jesus. The devotional climate has changed through the centuries. Karl Rahner, the great Jesuit theologian of the last century, had the insight that all devotion to Mary is tinged with the culture of the era. In the early church, Mary represented ascetic restrained spirituality. Mary, ever virgin, was a refined, controlled beauty.

In the later medieval times Mary was depicted as a romantic and courtly beauty, reminiscent of the regal themes of the times. The Gothic cathedrals reflect the richness of this tradition. The mysteries of the Rosary recall her life and her importance in the life of Jesus. The rosary beads were not only a great prayer tool, but a wonderful catechetical instrument. People learned their faith by praying the Rosary. The visual arts adorned her in rich jewels befitting the courtly presence of the patrons of the arts. Mary was thought of as a "softer" foil to Jesus, the judge and king.

Our Lady of Guadalupe is said to have appeared in 1531 to Juan Diego near Mexico City. The apparition combined a "European" Madonna with cultural elements of the indigenous Indian people, who regarded her as the feminine aspect of God. As Juan Diego depicted Mary she was very human, but her whole demeanor radiated divinity.

In the late nineteenth and early to mid-twentieth centuries, Mary was again idealized, placed high on a pedestal, clothed in beauty above the fray of the world. Apparitions at Lourdes and Fatima tended both to privatize and highlight devotion to Mary. In both of these situations designated individuals saw her and revealed her presence to others. At Lourdes (France) in 1858, Bernadette told of how Mary identified herself as the Immaculate Conception. Bernadette was instructed by Mary to bathe in a spring that had formed near the spot of the apparition. Ever since, the waters at Lourdes have been associated with many healings. At Fatima (Portugal) in 1917 Mary appeared to Lucia, Francisco, and Jacinta and called for penance, recitation of the Rosary, and devotion to the Immaculate Heart of Mary. These private revelations became known world-wide and were the source of increased devotion to Mary.

Two dogmas about Mary have been proclaimed in the last one hundred and fifty years. In 1854 Pope Pius IX defined the dogma of the Immaculate Conception, which holds that Mary was conceived without original sin. In other words, Mary's life was bonded to God's grace from the moment of her conception, thanks to the redeeming action of her son, Jesus Christ. In 1950 Pope Pius XII defined the dogma of the Assumption, which states that

Mary's body and soul were united with God in heaven. In other words, her whole person is with God, which is the great hope of all of us. These two dogmas tended to put Mary in a "privileged state" far above the rest of us.

One of the heated debates of the Second Vatican Council dealt with Mary's role in the church. Was it the "privileged" role apart from the faithful, or was it as a role model among the community of the faithful? In a close vote the decision was made to include a chapter on Mary in the Dogmatic Constitution on the Church. Mary is seen as the faithful responder to God's call. Because Mary said yes to being the mother of Jesus, God's plan for the incarnation happened. Mary is held in high esteem in the church. "The Church, therefore, in her apostolic work too, rightly looks to her [Mary] in order that through the Church he [Christ] could be born and increase in the hearts of the faithful. In her life the Virgin has been a model of that motherly love with which all who join in the Church's apostolic mission for the regeneration of humanity should be animated" (Dogmatic Constitution on the Church # 65).

We pray to Mary that we might be effective catechists, and that we might help our students pray to and with Mary as a member of the communion of saints. Marian prayer is a rewarding experience.

PRAYING AS THE CATECHIST

Reflect upon how difficult the decision must have been for Mary to say yes to being the mother of Jesus. She was engaged, but unmarried. Premarital sex was a disgrace, and if Mary were pregnant and unmarried, the conclusion would be that she had had sexual relations with Joseph. Joseph was bewildered. He knew that he had not had sex with Mary, and yet she was pregnant. When Mary said yes, she was accepting the possibility of a great deal of misunderstanding and negative judgment from many in the community. But God allayed Joseph's fears. Mary's yes transformed Joseph into a more faith-filled participant in God's plan. Mary's yes made the incarnation possible.

Light a candle. Recall the presence of the Holy Spirit in your midst—the same Holy Spirit who so deeply changed the life of Mary and empowered her to be the mother of Jesus. Slowly pray Mary's response to Elizabeth, her "Magnificat" (Luke 1:46–55).

Quietly pray again the first sentence of Mary's prayer. How has your soul magnified the Lord? How does your spirit rejoice in God your savior? How has God looked with favor on you? How are you "magnifying the Lord" as a catechist?

HELPING YOUNG CHILDREN TO PRAY

1. Place a picture or statue of Mary for the children to view. Explain that Mary is very special because she is the mother of Jesus. Talk about how God spoke to Mary through an angel, a messenger from God, and asked her to be Jesus' mother. Mary said yes. When Jesus grew up he told people about God his Father

and he helped people to see how God wants us to live. Jesus invites us to be his brothers and sisters.

2. Explain how Mary knew what God wanted her to do. Ask how we know what God wants of us. Do our parents, teachers, grandparents, and catechists help us to know what God wants of us? Talk about how God gave us a great gift in Jesus and that Jesus taught us how God wants us to live. Jesus taught us to be kind to others, to care for others, to be nice, to help other people, not to fight, not to be selfish, and so on.

3. The special prayer that the church prays to Mary is, as they know, called the Hail Mary. Teach the first part of the prayer, phrase by phrase, using gestures. Use the following chart to get started. Depending upon the age of the children, teaching the first part might be sufficient at this time. Pray the first part with gestures before teaching the second part.

Phrase	Interpretation	Gestures
Hail Mary	Greetings, Mary, *or* Hello, Mary	Arms outstretched high
Full of Grace	Full of God's love	Arms crossed over chest
The Lord is with you	Jesus is with you	Arms lowered

| Blessed are you among women | You are a very special mother | Arms crossed over chest |
| And blessed is the fruit of your womb | Because you are the mother of Jesus | Keep arms crossed over chest and bow head |

When it is appropriate to teach the second part of the Hail Mary, use the following as a guide.

Phrase	Interpretation	Gestures
Holy Mary, Mother of God	You are holy because you said yes to becoming Jesus' mother	Arms out-stretched high
Pray for us sinners	Help us when we are not being good	Arms crossed over chest
Now and at the hour of our death.	Always be willing to help us with your prayer	Arms lowered, head bowed
Amen.	We all agree to this	Arms crossed over chest

4. Prepare for and implement the prayer service.
- Quiet the children and pray reflective music in the background, such as "Hail Mary, Gentle Woman."
- Begin by praying the Sign of the Cross.
- Invite the children to sit in a circle and close their eyes as you pray the Opening Prayer: God, our creator and our Father, we thank you for giving us Mary as our mother and Jesus as our brother. We ask you to help us be like them and to love everyone we know. We ask this in Jesus' name through the power of the Holy Spirit.
  All: Amen.
- Proclaim the reading: Luke 1:26–28.
- Invite the children to close their eyes and thank God in their hearts for giving us his Son Jesus to show us how much he loves us, and for giving us Mary to be a mother to us also.
- As a sign of our gratitude to God, let us pray our Mary prayer. Have the children stand and pray the Hail Mary with gestures.
- Conclude the prayer service by singing a song the children know.

HELPING MIDDLE-GRADE CHILDREN TO PRAY

1. Before you begin this session, be sure you have at least one set of rosary beads to use for demonstra-

tion. Ideally it would be nice to have rosary beads for each child. Middle-grade children are often methodical and find the Rosary an interesting and orderly method of prayer. Tell them that before many people could read or write in the twelfth century, they often learned about Jesus and Mary by praying the Rosary. Ask them how many of them have prayed the Rosary before. If they have, now is a good time to review the process. If they have no knowledge of the Rosary, slowly explain how it is prayed. Recall the Joyful Mysteries of the Rosary (Annunciation, Visitation, Nativity, Presentation, Finding Jesus in the Temple). Note how to pray a decade of the Rosary by praying ten Hail Marys while meditating on a mystery. You might refer them to the Web site: http://www. rosary-center.org. There they will find information about each mystery of the Rosary as well as detailed instructions on how to pray it.

2. Note that Pope John Paul II added the Luminous Mysteries to the Joyful, Sorrowful, and Glorious Mysteries of the Rosary. Put the names of the Luminous Mysteries on the board (the Baptism of the Lord, the Wedding Feast at Cana, the Proclamation of the Kingdom, the Transfiguration, the Institution of the Eucharist). These are all based on events in the life of Jesus.

3. Discuss each one of the Luminous Mysteries with the children. What do we learn about Jesus in the following passages?

The Baptism of the Lord: Matt 3:13–17; Mark 1:1–11; John 1:29–34

The Wedding Feast at Cana: John 2:1–12

The Proclamation of the Kingdom: Matt 5:1–11, 13–16; Mark 1:14–15; Mark 4:21–32

The Transfiguration: Matt 17:1–8; Mark 9:2–8

The Institution of the Eucharist: Matt 26:20–30; Mark 14:17–26; John 13:21–30

4. Divide the children into five small groups and assign each group a Luminous Mystery to study. Have them do one of the following: prepare a skit based on the mystery; design a Web page based on the mystery; select a hymn that reflects the mystery well; or write a headline that announces the mystery.

5. Invite the groups to do a presentation based on their reflection.

6. Prepare for and implement the prayer service.

   - Have one group select appropriate music for the prayer service.
   - Have another group select and prepare one Bible reading for each mystery.
   - Invite another group to prepare the prayer environment.
   - Invite another group to be the prayer leaders for praying the Luminous Mysteries. (If your group has younger children, you may want to pray only one decade of the Rosary.)
   - Begin with the selected hymn.

- Prayer leaders begin with the initial prayers of the Rosary: Sign of the Cross, Apostles' Creed, Our Father, three Hail Marys, one Glory Be. Before each decade proclaim the Scripture passage chosen in #8 above.
- When all the decades are finished, close with another verse of the chosen hymn.

HELPING ADOLESCENTS TO PRAY

1. Review Mary's role in our belief system. Highlight that she
   - is the mother of Jesus, who is God's Son
   - was faithful to God's Word
   - was willing to take risks at God's request
   - was a caring person (visited Elizabeth, the wedding at Cana, etc.)
   - was given to us as our mother by Christ on the cross
   - is a role model for fidelity
   - is our advocate and our helper
   - is revered by the church
2. Discuss that historically people have felt that Mary was a great advocate for them. They knew how close she was to Jesus and tended to go to Mary to ask her to intercede for them with Christ. One prayer to Mary that has been prayed over the centuries is the *Memorare*. It is attributed to St. Bernard of Clairvaux (1090–1153).

3. Have copies of the prayer for each participant or put it on the board:

> Remember, O most gracious Virgin Mary, that never was it known that anyone who fled to your protection, implored your help, or sought your intercession was left unaided. Inspired by this confidence, we fly unto you, O Virgin of virgins, our Mother. To you we come, before you we stand, sinful and sorrowful. O Mother of the Word Incarnate, despise not our petitions but in your mercy, hear and answer us. Amen.

Discuss each sentence of the *Memorare* with the young people, breaking the prayer open so it connects with their lives. Let them paraphrase each sentence of the prayer in their own words. The first might sound something like this: "Mary, you are always there for people. You never say no when someone needs your help." The second sentence of the prayer might go like this: "Mary, we are really counting on you to help us." The third sentence might read: "We are at your doorstep, even though we have screwed up by sinning." The last sentence might be: "As the mother of Christ, show us mercy and help us. We really need it."

The point of this exercise is to help the young people see that this prayer to Mary is very intimate. It is prayed to a Mary they can know and count on, who knows them and loves them, who is very close to Christ, and is someone they can trust with their secrets.

4. Distribute at least one slip of paper to each participant. Ask them to write down one petition or concern they would bring to Mary. Try to help them see that they can pray for more than "things." Encourage them to pray for help in resolving a difficult problem, or for assistance in making decisions about the future, or for a special insight, or for the courage to stick with their convictions, or for the welfare of another person. Tell them they will not be asked to read their petitions out loud.

5. Prepare for and implement the prayer service.
   - Assign several young people to choose appropriate music.
   - Invite a group to select a reading such as:
     Luke 1:26–38; Luke 1:39–45; Luke 1:46–56; Luke 2:1–24.
   - Open with the selected hymn.
   - Pray or have one of the young people pray the Opening Prayer:
     God, our Father and creator, you have given us the gift of the mother of Jesus, your Son. Enable us to pray often to Mary and ask her to intercede for us as we continue to try to be faithful disciples of your Son, Jesus Christ. We are grateful for Mary's presence in our lives and hope to follow her example of fidelity to your Word. Be with us as we

strive to build your reign on earth. We ask this through Jesus Christ our Lord.
All: Amen.

- Stand and sing an Alleluia known to the group (e.g., Celtic Alleluia).
- Proclaim the gospel selected from the citations above.
- Allow for quiet reflection.
- Invite the young people to place their petitions to Mary in a decorated box near a lighted candle and the Bible.
- Pray the *Memorare* as a group.
- Exchange a sign of peace.
- Close with the final hymn.

7

Being a Disciple

IMMERSED IN FAITH

Discipleship is at the heart of the New Testament. To be a disciple of Jesus is to be his follower. The word *disciple* is found in the gospels and Acts of the Apostles at least 250 times. Disciples are bonded to one another and to Jesus. They learn from him and begin to act as he did.

True disciples do not choose Jesus; he chooses them. It is at his initiative that they are called. During his ministry on earth, Jesus wanted his disciples to do two things: to be with him in his ministry and to go out to teach and serve in his name. He wanted them to assist him in bringing about the reign of God.

Jesus was very inclusive in his call. In the Jewish tradition it was not unusual for rabbis to have disciples, but there were qualifications for this kind of discipleship. The followers had to be "ritually pure and religiously obedient." Jesus, on the other hand, included tax collectors and sinners as his disciples. Women also followed Jesus (Luke 8:2), which was counter-cultural at the time.

Jesus' call to discipleship demands a change in lifestyle. It is a radical conversion. Jesus asks his disciples to "see" life differently—to see it from the perspective of building the reign of God on earth, not building an earthly kingdom. Jesus asked his disciples to go beyond the requirements of the law and leave what they cherished for the sake of something bigger and better—God's reign on earth.

Jesus' disciples were called to serve the community in much the same way Jesus did. They were commissioned to cure the sick, to cast out demons, and to spread the good news that all are part of a people created, loved, and cherished by God. In serving others, disciples are called to share all they have. They are truly to be the epitome of those who "love one another as I have loved you" (John 15:12–13).

Jesus never promises that being a disciple will be easy. He challenges his disciples to "take up their cross and follow me," even if it means giving up one's life for another (Mark 8:34–35).

Being a disciple affects all areas of life. It is not just a job, it is an attitude. It is a life of action that reflects Jesus Christ. It is assuming the mindset of Jesus and following his instincts. The good news is that we have the Spirit in our midst to help us know what Jesus' instincts are and what his expectations are for us, his disciples in the twenty-first century.

Catechizing is certainly one of the ministries of discipleship. The *General Directory for Catechesis* calls catechesis an "apprenticeship in Christian life" (GDC 67). It "comprises more than mere instruction" (GDC 68). Catechesis "strengthens faith by developing a life in harmony with the Spirit of Christ…and encourages people to take an active part in the apostolate" (GDC 84).

Carefully attending to our own prayer lives enables us to help those we catechize grow in faith and prayerfulness, uniting them with Jesus Christ and fostering their development as disciples.

PRAYING AS THE CATECHIST

Reflect upon your call at baptism to be a disciple of Christ. Light a candle to remind you of the candle that was given to you at your baptism, which recalls Christ, the Light of the World. How have you grown in that vocation? What have you learned about yourself in the process? Which of the elements of discipleship, described above, have you fully embraced? Which ones are a struggle for you? How do you see the relationship between catechizing and discipleship? Use Luke 6:27–31 to reflect prayerfully on discipleship.

HELPING YOUNG CHILDREN TO PRAY

1. Explain that a disciple is a follower of Jesus—the disciples followed the teachings of Jesus, worked together to help people know Jesus, and did whatever Jesus asked of them. They cared for people and helped them when they could.

2. Ask the children what they think Jesus wants them to do to be a follower or a disciple. (Do good things for others; care for creation; obey parents and teachers; play nicely with others, etc.)

3. Distribute to each child a prepared 9 x 12 piece of construction paper which is labeled on the long side, "I am a follower of Jesus." With a marker, divide the sheet into four rectangles. Invite the children to draw four pictures of themselves following Jesus. If you are working with very young children, have them do just one drawing and use the entire sheet.

4. Walk around the classroom, encouraging the children as they draw. Informally reinforce the concept of discipleship with the children.

5. Prepare for and implement the prayer service.
   - Invite the children to sit in a circle. Have the candle lighted and the Bible open to the Scripture passage. Remind the children that we light the candle to remind us that Jesus is present with us as we pray.
   - Sing a refrain from a hymn that the children know.
   - Opening Prayer: God our loving Father, you have given us your Son, Jesus, to be with us. Jesus has invited us to be his followers. Help us be faithful followers of him. Enable us to help others even when we don't feel like it. We ask this in Jesus' name and through the power of the Holy Spirit. Amen.
   - Proclaim John 13:34–35.

- Invite the children to close their eyes and think about how much God loves them. And then thank God in their hearts for loving them.
- Litany of Thanksgiving:
The children should hold up their drawings and describe one of the ways they are being followers of Jesus. After each child shares, all respond: We thank you, Jesus, for giving us _____ (name of child).
- Close the prayer service by praying the Our Father.
- Sing a closing hymn known to the children.

HELPING MIDDLE-GRADE CHILDREN TO PRAY

1. Introduce the notion of discipleship by writing the four marks of discipleship on the board:
   - Disciples are called by Jesus (at baptism).
   - All people are invited to be disciples. We don't have to be perfect to be called to be a follower of Jesus.
   - Being a follower of Jesus means our whole life is dedicated to living the gospel. It is about praying and being in communion with Jesus. It is about how you treat others, and so on.
   - Discipleship means doing the things Jesus did. It means loving others with our whole self.
2. Discuss each of these with the young people. Allow the children to draw examples from their lives.

3. Divide the group into three and have each group design a "help-wanted" poster based on the qualifications of discipleship noted above. Encourage them to use contemporary language that would appeal to people their own age.

4. Invite each group to display their poster and discuss who would be attracted to the kind of discipleship they portrayed on the poster.

5. Use the posters in the prayer environment and later display them in a prominent place where parishioners can see them.

6. Prepare for and implement the prayer service.
   - Have several young people select music from a parish hymnal related to discipleship, such as "Bring Forth the Kingdom" or "City of God."
   - Invite some of them to make up general intercessions related to the theme.
   - Select one student to proclaim the reading noted below.
   - Open with the selected hymn.
   - Opening Prayer: God, our loving Father and creator, be with us as we try to learn to be disciples of your Son, Jesus Christ. Enable us to be recognized as his followers by our actions and our words. Strengthen us when we feel too lazy to care for others, or when we are too tired to be open to other people. Help us to follow you by obeying our parents and teachers. We ask this through

Christ, our Lord and brother, and the Holy Spirit, who dwells in us.

All: Amen.

- Proclaim the gospel (Matt 5:43–45a, 46a, 48).
- Invite the children to pray in their hearts, using the questions below to reflect. Tell them they will not be sharing the answers to these questions, but they should talk to God in their hearts about the answers. Have them close their eyes. Play quiet, reflective music, if possible. Read the questions slowly, allowing time for reflection between each one.
    (a) Who are your enemies? What can you do to show you love them?
    (b) Do others ever pick on you or try to hurt your feelings? Who? How?
    (c) How and when can you pray for those who do this to you? What is hard about this? Is this truly what Jesus wants of his disciples?
    (d) Close your meditation by telling Jesus in your heart what you will do to love your enemies.
- Pray the general intercessions prepared by the young people.

    Response: Lord hear our prayer.
- Pray the Lord's Prayer together.
- Exchange a sign of peace.
- Sing the closing hymn.

HELPING ADOLESCENTS TO PRAY

1. Introduce the theme of discipleship by asking the young people to name heroes and heroines in their lives. These people may be music idols, film stars, sports heroes, and the like. Ask what attracts them to these people. Probe the influence the "stars" have on their lives. Ask what it is about the stars that they admire? What aspects of their own lives would they like to be similar to their heroes and heroines?

2. Transition into the topic of being a disciple of Jesus Christ. Ask what they most admire about Jesus. How is Jesus different from their contemporary heroes and heroines? How is he the same?

3. Provide the young people with New Testaments. Divide them into small groups and assign each group several scriptural citations to find and reflect upon. Ask them to discover what Jesus' expectations of disciples are. Possible references: Matthew 4:25; Matthew 8:1; Mark 1:18; Luke 5:11; John 1:43; Mark 10:21; Luke 14:26; Luke 10:2–12; Luke 6:30; Mark 9:35; Matthew 5:38–42; John 15:12–13.

4. After the young people have studied the Scripture passages, invite each group to design a job description for a teenage disciple under the following headings: Major Responsibilities of the Position; Skills and Knowledge Required for the Position; Job Training; Accountability; and so forth. Note that many of the

apostles were probably teens or young people when they said yes to following Jesus.

5. Have each small group make a presentation on the job description they have designed. Compare and contrast the job descriptions produced by the groups. Then have each person quietly list the job responsibilities they could fulfill and those that would be the hardest to do. Invite each person to pray quietly and ask Jesus to strengthen him or her in one area of the job description where they wish to grow stronger. Allow quiet time for this. Play reflective music as the group does this.

6. Prepare for and implement the prayer service.
   - Divide the young people into four groups, asking each group to do one of the following:
     - (a) Select music for the beginning and end of the prayer service such as "*Somos el Cuerpo de Cristo/* We Are the Body of Christ" or "God Has Chosen Me."
     - (b) Write general intercessions related to discipleship.
     - (c) Select and prepare the readings for the prayer service: consider using some of the citations noted above.
     - (d) Create a prayerful environment around the theme of discipleship.
   - Begin with the opening song.
   - Opening Prayer: God, our Father and creator, inspire us to be disciples of your Son, Jesus Christ.

Empower us to begin to think like him, act like him, and pray like him. Encourage us through the power of the Holy Spirit when we get discouraged with the way we are handling life. Bond us with your Son as we struggle to be his faithful disciples. We ask this through Jesus Christ and the Holy Spirit.

All: Amen.

- Proclamation of the Word of God as selected above.
- Silent reflection.
- General intercessions.
- Anointing for Discipleship.

  As a symbol of our renewed commitment to our baptism each person is invited to come forward and have his or her hand signed with the cross in oil. (The catechist should have a small glass bowl of olive oil. The catechist will then mark each person's hand with the sign of the cross, saying, "May you be a strong disciple of Jesus Christ." Each person responds "Amen.")
- All pray the Lord's Prayer.
- Close with the final stanza of the song chosen above.

OTHER BOOKS IN THIS SERIES

Connecting with Parents
Mary Twomey Spollen

Teaching the Faith
Kim Duty